Address Book

This Address Book Belongs To:

E-mail:

Phone:

Important Phone Numbers

Contact	Phone #

Important Dates

Date	Occasion/Event

A

Name

Address

Phone   Cell
Office   Fax
Email

Name

Address

Phone   Cell
Office   Fax
Email

Name

Address

Phone   Cell
Office   Fax
Email

Name

Address

Phone   Cell
Office   Fax
Email

Name

Address

Phone   Cell
Office   Fax
Email

Name

Address

Phone   Cell
Office   Fax
Email

Name

Address

Phone   Cell
Office   Fax
Email

Name

Address

Phone   Cell
Office   Fax
Email

Name

Address

Phone   Cell
Office   Fax
Email

Name

Address

Phone   Cell
Office   Fax
Email

Strive not to be a success, but rather to be of value. –Albert Einstein

A

Name	*Name*
Address	*Address*
Phone　　　*Cell*	*Phone*　　　*Cell*
Office　　　*Fax*	*Office*　　　*Fax*
Email	*Email*

Name	*Name*
Address	*Address*
Phone　　　*Cell*	*Phone*　　　*Cell*
Office　　　*Fax*	*Office*　　　*Fax*
Email	*Email*

Name	*Name*
Address	*Address*
Phone　　　*Cell*	*Phone*　　　*Cell*
Office　　　*Fax*	*Office*　　　*Fax*
Email	*Email*

Name	*Name*
Address	*Address*
Phone　　　*Cell*	*Phone*　　　*Cell*
Office　　　*Fax*	*Office*　　　*Fax*
Email	*Email*

Name	*Name*
Address	*Address*
Phone　　　*Cell*	*Phone*　　　*Cell*
Office　　　*Fax*	*Office*　　　*Fax*
Email	*Email*

The only person you are destined to become is the person you decide to be.
–Ralph Waldo Emerson

A

Name
Address

Phone | Cell
Office | Fax
Email

Name
Address

Phone | Cell
Office | Fax
Email

Name
Address

Phone | Cell
Office | Fax
Email

Name
Address

Phone | Cell
Office | Fax
Email

Name
Address

Phone | Cell
Office | Fax
Email

Name
Address

Phone | Cell
Office | Fax
Email

Name
Address

Phone | Cell
Office | Fax
Email

Name
Address

Phone | Cell
Office | Fax
Email

Name
Address

Phone | Cell
Office | Fax
Email

Name
Address

Phone | Cell
Office | Fax
Email

Optimism is the one quality more associated with success and happiness than any other. –Brian Tracy

A

Name	*Name*
Address	*Address*
Phone *Cell*	*Phone* *Cell*
Office *Fax*	*Office* *Fax*
Email	*Email*
Name	*Name*
Address	*Address*
Phone *Cell*	*Phone* *Cell*
Office *Fax*	*Office* *Fax*
Email	*Email*
Name	*Name*
Address	*Address*
Phone *Cell*	*Phone* *Cell*
Office *Fax*	*Office* *Fax*
Email	*Email*
Name	*Name*
Address	*Address*
Phone *Cell*	*Phone* *Cell*
Office *Fax*	*Office* *Fax*
Email	*Email*
Name	*Name*
Address	*Address*
Phone *Cell*	*Phone* *Cell*
Office *Fax*	*Office* *Fax*
Email	*Email*

But if we use our imaginations, our possibilities become limitless. –Jamie Paolinetti

A

Name	Name
Address	Address

Phone	Cell	Phone	Cell
Office	Fax	Office	Fax
Email		Email	

Name	Name
Address	Address

Phone	Cell	Phone	Cell
Office	Fax	Office	Fax
Email		Email	

Name	Name
Address	Address

Phone	Cell	Phone	Cell
Office	Fax	Office	Fax
Email		Email	

Name	Name
Address	Address

Phone	Cell	Phone	Cell
Office	Fax	Office	Fax
Email		Email	

Name	Name
Address	Address

Phone	Cell	Phone	Cell
Office	Fax	Office	Fax
Email		Email	

Life shrinks or expands in proportion to one's courage. –Anais Nin

B

Name

Address

Phone   *Cell*

Office   *Fax*

Email

Name

Address

Phone   *Cell*

Office   *Fax*

Email

Name

Address

Phone   *Cell*

Office   *Fax*

Email

Name

Address

Phone   *Cell*

Office   *Fax*

Email

Name

Address

Phone   *Cell*

Office   *Fax*

Email

Name

Address

Phone   *Cell*

Office   *Fax*

Email

Name

Address

Phone   *Cell*

Office   *Fax*

Email

Name

Address

Phone   *Cell*

Office   *Fax*

Email

Name

Address

Phone   *Cell*

Office   *Fax*

Email

Name

Address

Phone   *Cell*

Office   *Fax*

Email

Friendship is certainly the finest balm for the pangs of disappointed love.
- Jane Austen

Name

Address

Phone   *Cell*

Office   *Fax*

Email

Name

Address

Phone   *Cell*

Office   *Fax*

Email

Name

Address

Phone   *Cell*

Office   *Fax*

Email

Name

Address

Phone   *Cell*

Office   *Fax*

Email

Name

Address

Phone   *Cell*

Office   *Fax*

Email

Name

Address

Phone   *Cell*

Office   *Fax*

Email

Name

Address

Phone   *Cell*

Office   *Fax*

Email

Name

Address

Phone   *Cell*

Office   *Fax*

Email

Name

Address

Phone   *Cell*

Office   *Fax*

Email

Name

Address

Phone   *Cell*

Office   *Fax*

Email

Remember that the most valuable antiques are dear old friends.
- H. Jackson Brown, Jr.

B

Name

Address

Phone	*Cell*
Office	*Fax*
Email	

Name

Address

Phone	*Cell*
Office	*Fax*
Email	

Name

Address

Phone	*Cell*
Office	*Fax*
Email	

Name

Address

Phone	*Cell*
Office	*Fax*
Email	

Name

Address

Phone	*Cell*
Office	*Fax*
Email	

Name

Address

Phone	*Cell*
Office	*Fax*
Email	

Name

Address

Phone	*Cell*
Office	*Fax*
Email	

Name

Address

Phone	*Cell*
Office	*Fax*
Email	

Name

Address

Phone	*Cell*
Office	*Fax*
Email	

Name

Address

Phone	*Cell*
Office	*Fax*
Email	

True friendship is when two friends can walk in opposite directions, yet remain side by side.

B

Name

Address

Phone   Cell

Office   Fax

Email

Name

Address

Phone   Cell

Office   Fax

Email

Name

Address

Phone   Cell

Office   Fax

Email

Name

Address

Phone   Cell

Office   Fax

Email

Name

Address

Phone   Cell

Office   Fax

Email

Name

Address

Phone   Cell

Office   Fax

Email

Name

Address

Phone   Cell

Office   Fax

Email

Name

Address

Phone   Cell

Office   Fax

Email

Name

Address

Phone   Cell

Office   Fax

Email

Name

Address

Phone   Cell

Office   Fax

Email

Whatever the mind of man can conceive and believe, it can achieve. --Napoleon Hill

C

Name

Address

Phone   *Cell*

Office   *Fax*

Email

Name

Address

Phone   *Cell*

Office   *Fax*

Email

Name

Address

Phone   *Cell*

Office   *Fax*

Email

Name

Address

Phone   *Cell*

Office   *Fax*

Email

Name

Address

Phone   *Cell*

Office   *Fax*

Email

Name

Address

Phone   *Cell*

Office   *Fax*

Email

Name

Address

Phone   *Cell*

Office   *Fax*

Email

Name

Address

Phone   *Cell*

Office   *Fax*

Email

Name

Address

Phone   *Cell*

Office   *Fax*

Email

Name

Address

Phone   *Cell*

Office   *Fax*

Email

A friend is someone who can see the truth and pain in you even when you are fooling everyone else.

Name

Address

Phone   *Cell*

Office   *Fax*

Email

Name

Address

Phone   *Cell*

Office   *Fax*

Email

Name

Address

Phone   *Cell*

Office   *Fax*

Email

Name

Address

Phone   *Cell*

Office   *Fax*

Email

Name

Address

Phone   *Cell*

Office   *Fax*

Email

Name

Address

Phone   *Cell*

Office   *Fax*

Email

Name

Address

Phone   *Cell*

Office   *Fax*

Email

Name

Address

Phone   *Cell*

Office   *Fax*

Email

Name

Address

Phone   *Cell*

Office   *Fax*

Email

Name

Address

Phone   *Cell*

Office   *Fax*

Email

Explore, Dream, Discover. –Mark Twain

C

Name		Name	
Address		*Address*	
Phone	*Cell*	*Phone*	*Cell*
Office	*Fax*	*Office*	*Fax*
Email		*Email*	

Name		Name	
Address		*Address*	
Phone	*Cell*	*Phone*	*Cell*
Office	*Fax*	*Office*	*Fax*
Email		*Email*	

Name		Name	
Address		*Address*	
Phone	*Cell*	*Phone*	*Cell*
Office	*Fax*	*Office*	*Fax*
Email		*Email*	

Name		Name	
Address		*Address*	
Phone	*Cell*	*Phone*	*Cell*
Office	*Fax*	*Office*	*Fax*
Email		*Email*	

Name		Name	
Address		*Address*	
Phone	*Cell*	*Phone*	*Cell*
Office	*Fax*	*Office*	*Fax*
Email		*Email*	

The friendship that can cease has never been real.
- St. Jerome

Name

Address

Phone *Cell*

Office *Fax*

Email

Name

Address

Phone *Cell*

Office *Fax*

Email

Name

Address

Phone *Cell*

Office *Fax*

Email

Name

Address

Phone *Cell*

Office *Fax*

Email

Name

Address

Phone *Cell*

Office *Fax*

Email

Name

Address

Phone *Cell*

Office *Fax*

Email

Name

Address

Phone *Cell*

Office *Fax*

Email

Name

Address

Phone *Cell*

Office *Fax*

Email

Name

Address

Phone *Cell*

Office *Fax*

Email

Name

Address

Phone *Cell*

Office *Fax*

Email

If you're offered a seat on a rocket ship, don't ask what seat! Just get on.
–Sheryl Sandberg

D

Name

Address

Phone   *Cell*

Office   *Fax*

Email

Name

Address

Phone   *Cell*

Office   *Fax*

Email

Name

Address

Phone   *Cell*

Office   *Fax*

Email

Name

Address

Phone   *Cell*

Office   *Fax*

Email

Name

Address

Phone   *Cell*

Office   *Fax*

Email

Name

Address

Phone   *Cell*

Office   *Fax*

Email

Name

Address

Phone   *Cell*

Office   *Fax*

Email

Name

Address

Phone   *Cell*

Office   *Fax*

Email

Name

Address

Phone   *Cell*

Office   *Fax*

Email

Name

Address

Phone   *Cell*

Office   *Fax*

Email

Certain things catch your eye, but pursue only those that capture the heart. –
Ancient Indian Proverb

D

Name
Address

Phone   *Cell*
Office   *Fax*
Email

Name
Address

Phone   *Cell*
Office   *Fax*
Email

Name
Address

Phone   *Cell*
Office   *Fax*
Email

Name
Address

Phone   *Cell*
Office   *Fax*
Email

Name
Address

Phone   *Cell*
Office   *Fax*
Email

Name
Address

Phone   *Cell*
Office   *Fax*
Email

Name
Address

Phone   *Cell*
Office   *Fax*
Email

Name
Address

Phone   *Cell*
Office   *Fax*
Email

Name
Address

Phone   *Cell*
Office   *Fax*
Email

Name
Address

Phone   *Cell*
Office   *Fax*
Email

Live the life you have imagined. –Henry David Thoreau

D

Name

Address

Phone　　　　　　*Cell*

Office　　　　　　*Fax*

Email

Name

Address

Phone　　　　　　*Cell*

Office　　　　　　*Fax*

Email

Name

Address

Phone　　　　　　*Cell*

Office　　　　　　*Fax*

Email

Name

Address

Phone　　　　　　*Cell*

Office　　　　　　*Fax*

Email

Name

Address

Phone　　　　　　*Cell*

Office　　　　　　*Fax*

Email

Name

Address

Phone　　　　　　*Cell*

Office　　　　　　*Fax*

Email

Name

Address

Phone　　　　　　*Cell*

Office　　　　　　*Fax*

Email

Name

Address

Phone　　　　　　*Cell*

Office　　　　　　*Fax*

Email

Name

Address

Phone　　　　　　*Cell*

Office　　　　　　*Fax*

Email

Name

Address

Phone　　　　　　*Cell*

Office　　　　　　*Fax*

Email

Either you run the day, or the day runs you. –Jim Rohn

Name	*Name*
Address	*Address*
Phone *Cell*	*Phone* *Cell*
Office *Fax*	*Office* *Fax*
Email	*Email*
Name	*Name*
Address	*Address*
Phone *Cell*	*Phone* *Cell*
Office *Fax*	*Office* *Fax*
Email	*Email*
Name	*Name*
Address	*Address*
Phone *Cell*	*Phone* *Cell*
Office *Fax*	*Office* *Fax*
Email	*Email*
Name	*Name*
Address	*Address*
Phone *Cell*	*Phone* *Cell*
Office *Fax*	*Office* *Fax*
Email	*Email*
Name	*Name*
Address	*Address*
Phone *Cell*	*Phone* *Cell*
Office *Fax*	*Office* *Fax*
Email	*Email*

If you do what you've always done, you'll get what you've always gotten. –Tony Robbins

Name

Address

Phone   *Cell*

Office   *Fax*

Email

Name

Address

Phone   *Cell*

Office   *Fax*

Email

Name

Address

Phone   *Cell*

Office   *Fax*

Email

Name

Address

Phone   *Cell*

Office   *Fax*

Email

Name

Address

Phone   *Cell*

Office   *Fax*

Email

Name

Address

Phone   *Cell*

Office   *Fax*

Email

Name

Address

Phone   *Cell*

Office   *Fax*

Email

Name

Address

Phone   *Cell*

Office   *Fax*

Email

Name

Address

Phone   *Cell*

Office   *Fax*

Email

Name

Address

Phone   *Cell*

Office   *Fax*

Email

Friendship is like peeing your pants. Everyone can see, but only you can feel its warmth.

E

Name	*Name*
Address	*Address*
Phone *Cell*	*Phone* *Cell*
Office *Fax*	*Office* *Fax*
Email	*Email*
Name	*Name*
Address	*Address*
Phone *Cell*	*Phone* *Cell*
Office *Fax*	*Office* *Fax*
Email	*Email*
Name	*Name*
Address	*Address*
Phone *Cell*	*Phone* *Cell*
Office *Fax*	*Office* *Fax*
Email	*Email*
Name	*Name*
Address	*Address*
Phone *Cell*	*Phone* *Cell*
Office *Fax*	*Office* *Fax*
Email	*Email*
Name	*Name*
Address	*Address*
Phone *Cell*	*Phone* *Cell*
Office *Fax*	*Office* *Fax*
Email	*Email*

There is nothing on this earth more to be prized than true friendship.
- Thomas Aquinas

E

Name	*Name*
Address	*Address*
Phone *Cell*	*Phone* *Cell*
Office *Fax*	*Office* *Fax*
Email	*Email*

Name	*Name*
Address	*Address*
Phone *Cell*	*Phone* *Cell*
Office *Fax*	*Office* *Fax*
Email	*Email*

Name	*Name*
Address	*Address*
Phone *Cell*	*Phone* *Cell*
Office *Fax*	*Office* *Fax*
Email	*Email*

Name	*Name*
Address	*Address*
Phone *Cell*	*Phone* *Cell*
Office *Fax*	*Office* *Fax*
Email	*Email*

Name	*Name*
Address	*Address*
Phone *Cell*	*Phone* *Cell*
Office *Fax*	*Office* *Fax*
Email	*Email*

But there's no joy in living your whole life on the ground. –Unknown

Name

Address

Phone   Cell

Office   Fax

Email

Name

Address

Phone   Cell

Office   Fax

Email

Name

Address

Phone   Cell

Office   Fax

Email

Name

Address

Phone   Cell

Office   Fax

Email

Name

Address

Phone   Cell

Office   Fax

Email

Name

Address

Phone   Cell

Office   Fax

Email

Name

Address

Phone   Cell

Office   Fax

Email

Name

Address

Phone   Cell

Office   Fax

Email

Name

Address

Phone   Cell

Office   Fax

Email

Name

Address

Phone   Cell

Office   Fax

Email

Fall seven times and stand up eight. –Japanese Proverb

Name

Address

Phone   *Cell*
Office   *Fax*
Email

Name

Address

Phone   *Cell*
Office   *Fax*
Email

Name

Address

Phone   *Cell*
Office   *Fax*
Email

Name

Address

Phone   *Cell*
Office   *Fax*
Email

Name

Address

Phone   *Cell*
Office   *Fax*
Email

Name

Address

Phone   *Cell*
Office   *Fax*
Email

Name

Address

Phone   *Cell*
Office   *Fax*
Email

Name

Address

Phone   *Cell*
Office   *Fax*
Email

Name

Address

Phone   *Cell*
Office   *Fax*
Email

Name

Address

Phone   *Cell*
Office   *Fax*
Email

A truly rich man is one whose children run into his arms when his hands are empty. –Unknown

Name

Address

Phone   Cell
Office   Fax
Email

Name

Address

Phone   Cell
Office   Fax
Email

Name

Address

Phone   Cell
Office   Fax
Email

Name

Address

Phone   Cell
Office   Fax
Email

Name

Address

Phone   Cell
Office   Fax
Email

Name

Address

Phone   Cell
Office   Fax
Email

Name

Address

Phone   Cell
Office   Fax
Email

Name

Address

Phone   Cell
Office   Fax
Email

Name

Address

Phone   Cell
Office   Fax
Email

Name

Address

Phone   Cell
Office   Fax
Email

Dreaming, after all, is a form of planning. –Gloria Steinem

F

Name		Name	
Address		Address	
Phone	Cell	Phone	Cell
Office	Fax	Office	Fax
Email		Email	

Name		Name	
Address		Address	
Phone	Cell	Phone	Cell
Office	Fax	Office	Fax
Email		Email	

Name		Name	
Address		Address	
Phone	Cell	Phone	Cell
Office	Fax	Office	Fax
Email		Email	

Name		Name	
Address		Address	
Phone	Cell	Phone	Cell
Office	Fax	Office	Fax
Email		Email	

Name		Name	
Address		Address	
Phone	Cell	Phone	Cell
Office	Fax	Office	Fax
Email		Email	

I have learned over the years that when one's mind is made up, this diminishes fear. –Rosa Parks

F

Name	Name
Address	Address

Phone	Cell	Phone	Cell
Office	Fax	Office	Fax
Email		Email	

Name	Name
Address	Address

Phone	Cell	Phone	Cell
Office	Fax	Office	Fax
Email		Email	

Name	Name
Address	Address

Phone	Cell	Phone	Cell
Office	Fax	Office	Fax
Email		Email	

Name	Name
Address	Address

Phone	Cell	Phone	Cell
Office	Fax	Office	Fax
Email		Email	

Name	Name
Address	Address

Phone	Cell	Phone	Cell
Office	Fax	Office	Fax
Email		Email	

In order to succeed, your desire for success should be greater than your fear of failure. –Bill Cosby

F

Name

Address

Phone   *Cell*

Office   *Fax*

Email

Name

Address

Phone   *Cell*

Office   *Fax*

Email

Name

Address

Phone   *Cell*

Office   *Fax*

Email

Name

Address

Phone   *Cell*

Office   *Fax*

Email

Name

Address

Phone   *Cell*

Office   *Fax*

Email

Name

Address

Phone   *Cell*

Office   *Fax*

Email

Name

Address

Phone   *Cell*

Office   *Fax*

Email

Name

Address

Phone   *Cell*

Office   *Fax*

Email

Name

Address

Phone   *Cell*

Office   *Fax*

Email

Name

Address

Phone   *Cell*

Office   *Fax*

Email

Winning isn't everything, but wanting to win is. –Vince Lombardi

F

Name

Address

Phone   *Cell*

Office   *Fax*

Email

Name

Address

Phone   *Cell*

Office   *Fax*

Email

Name

Address

Phone   *Cell*

Office   *Fax*

Email

Name

Address

Phone   *Cell*

Office   *Fax*

Email

Name

Address

Phone   *Cell*

Office   *Fax*

Email

Name

Address

Phone   *Cell*

Office   *Fax*

Email

Name

Address

Phone   *Cell*

Office   *Fax*

Email

Name

Address

Phone   *Cell*

Office   *Fax*

Email

Name

Address

Phone   *Cell*

Office   *Fax*

Email

Name

Address

Phone   *Cell*

Office   *Fax*

Email

If you can dream it, you can achieve it. –Zig Ziglar

G

Name		*Name*	
Address		*Address*	
Phone	*Cell*	*Phone*	*Cell*
Office	*Fax*	*Office*	*Fax*
Email		*Email*	
Name		*Name*	
Address		*Address*	
Phone	*Cell*	*Phone*	*Cell*
Office	*Fax*	*Office*	*Fax*
Email		*Email*	
Name		*Name*	
Address		*Address*	
Phone	*Cell*	*Phone*	*Cell*
Office	*Fax*	*Office*	*Fax*
Email		*Email*	
Name		*Name*	
Address		*Address*	
Phone	*Cell*	*Phone*	*Cell*
Office	*Fax*	*Office*	*Fax*
Email		*Email*	
Name		*Name*	
Address		*Address*	
Phone	*Cell*	*Phone*	*Cell*
Office	*Fax*	*Office*	*Fax*
Email		*Email*	

I am not a product of my circumstances. I am a product of my decisions.
–Stephen Covey

Name	*Name*
Address	*Address*
Phone *Cell*	*Phone* *Cell*
Office *Fax*	*Office* *Fax*
Email	*Email*

Name	*Name*
Address	*Address*
Phone *Cell*	*Phone* *Cell*
Office *Fax*	*Office* *Fax*
Email	*Email*

Name	*Name*
Address	*Address*
Phone *Cell*	*Phone* *Cell*
Office *Fax*	*Office* *Fax*
Email	*Email*

Name	*Name*
Address	*Address*
Phone *Cell*	*Phone* *Cell*
Office *Fax*	*Office* *Fax*
Email	*Email*

Name	*Name*
Address	*Address*
Phone *Cell*	*Phone* *Cell*
Office *Fax*	*Office* *Fax*
Email	*Email*

If the wind will not serve, take to the oars. –Latin Proverb

G

Name

Address

Phone   *Cell*

Office   *Fax*

Email

Name

Address

Phone   *Cell*

Office   *Fax*

Email

Name

Address

Phone   *Cell*

Office   *Fax*

Email

Name

Address

Phone   *Cell*

Office   *Fax*

Email

Name

Address

Phone   *Cell*

Office   *Fax*

Email

Name

Address

Phone   *Cell*

Office   *Fax*

Email

Name

Address

Phone   *Cell*

Office   *Fax*

Email

Name

Address

Phone   *Cell*

Office   *Fax*

Email

Name

Address

Phone   *Cell*

Office   *Fax*

Email

Name

Address

Phone   *Cell*

Office   *Fax*

Email

You may be disappointed if you fail, but you are doomed if you don't try.
–Beverly Sills

G

Name	Name
Address	Address

Phone	Cell	Phone	Cell
Office	Fax	Office	Fax
Email		Email	

Name	Name
Address	Address

Phone	Cell	Phone	Cell
Office	Fax	Office	Fax
Email		Email	

Name	Name
Address	Address

Phone	Cell	Phone	Cell
Office	Fax	Office	Fax
Email		Email	

Name	Name
Address	Address

Phone	Cell	Phone	Cell
Office	Fax	Office	Fax
Email		Email	

Name	Name
Address	Address

Phone	Cell	Phone	Cell
Office	Fax	Office	Fax
Email		Email	

Whether you think you can or you think you can't, you're right. –Henry Ford

H

Name	*Name*
Address	*Address*
Phone *Cell*	*Phone* *Cell*
Office *Fax*	*Office* *Fax*
Email	*Email*

Name	*Name*
Address	*Address*
Phone *Cell*	*Phone* *Cell*
Office *Fax*	*Office* *Fax*
Email	*Email*

Name	*Name*
Address	*Address*
Phone *Cell*	*Phone* *Cell*
Office *Fax*	*Office* *Fax*
Email	*Email*

Name	*Name*
Address	*Address*
Phone *Cell*	*Phone* *Cell*
Office *Fax*	*Office* *Fax*
Email	*Email*

Name	*Name*
Address	*Address*
Phone *Cell*	*Phone* *Cell*
Office *Fax*	*Office* *Fax*
Email	*Email*

The question isn't who is going to let me; it's who is going to stop me. —Ayn Rand

Name

Address

Phone   *Cell*

Office   *Fax*

Email

Name

Address

Phone   *Cell*

Office   *Fax*

Email

Name

Address

Phone   *Cell*

Office   *Fax*

Email

Name

Address

Phone   *Cell*

Office   *Fax*

Email

Name

Address

Phone   *Cell*

Office   *Fax*

Email

Name

Address

Phone   *Cell*

Office   *Fax*

Email

Name

Address

Phone   *Cell*

Office   *Fax*

Email

Name

Address

Phone   *Cell*

Office   *Fax*

Email

Name

Address

Phone   *Cell*

Office   *Fax*

Email

Name

Address

Phone   *Cell*

Office   *Fax*

Email

I would rather die of passion than of boredom. –Vincent van Gogh

Name		Name	
Address		Address	
Phone	Cell	Phone	Cell
Office	Fax	Office	Fax
Email		Email	

Name		Name	
Address		Address	
Phone	Cell	Phone	Cell
Office	Fax	Office	Fax
Email		Email	

Name		Name	
Address		Address	
Phone	Cell	Phone	Cell
Office	Fax	Office	Fax
Email		Email	

Name		Name	
Address		Address	
Phone	Cell	Phone	Cell
Office	Fax	Office	Fax
Email		Email	

Name		Name	
Address		Address	
Phone	Cell	Phone	Cell
Office	Fax	Office	Fax
Email		Email	

Don't spend time beating on a wall, hoping to transform it into a door. –Coco Chanel

Name

Address

Phone   Cell
Office   Fax
Email

Name

Address

Phone   Cell
Office   Fax
Email

Name

Address

Phone   Cell
Office   Fax
Email

Name

Address

Phone   Cell
Office   Fax
Email

Name

Address

Phone   Cell
Office   Fax
Email

Name

Address

Phone   Cell
Office   Fax
Email

Name

Address

Phone   Cell
Office   Fax
Email

Name

Address

Phone   Cell
Office   Fax
Email

Name

Address

Phone   Cell
Office   Fax
Email

Name

Address

Phone   Cell
Office   Fax
Email

Never explain - your friends do not need it and your enemies will not believe you anyway. - Elbert Hubbard

I

Name

Address

Phone   *Cell*

Office   *Fax*

Email

Name

Address

Phone   *Cell*

Office   *Fax*

Email

Name

Address

Phone   *Cell*

Office   *Fax*

Email

Name

Address

Phone   *Cell*

Office   *Fax*

Email

Name

Address

Phone   *Cell*

Office   *Fax*

Email

Name

Address

Phone   *Cell*

Office   *Fax*

Email

Name

Address

Phone   *Cell*

Office   *Fax*

Email

Name

Address

Phone   *Cell*

Office   *Fax*

Email

Name

Address

Phone   *Cell*

Office   *Fax*

Email

Name

Address

Phone   *Cell*

Office   *Fax*

Email

The only way to do great work is to love what you do. –Steve Jobs

Name
Address

Phone   *Cell*
Office   *Fax*
Email

Name
Address

Phone   *Cell*
Office   *Fax*
Email

Name
Address

Phone   *Cell*
Office   *Fax*
Email

Name
Address

Phone   *Cell*
Office   *Fax*
Email

Name
Address

Phone   *Cell*
Office   *Fax*
Email

Name
Address

Phone   *Cell*
Office   *Fax*
Email

Name
Address

Phone   *Cell*
Office   *Fax*
Email

Name
Address

Phone   *Cell*
Office   *Fax*
Email

Name
Address

Phone   *Cell*
Office   *Fax*
Email

Name
Address

Phone   *Cell*
Office   *Fax*
Email

The most common way people give up their power is by thinking they don't have any. –Alice Walker

I

Name	Name
Address	Address
Phone Cell	Phone Cell
Office Fax	Office Fax
Email	Email

Name	Name
Address	Address
Phone Cell	Phone Cell
Office Fax	Office Fax
Email	Email

Name	Name
Address	Address
Phone Cell	Phone Cell
Office Fax	Office Fax
Email	Email

Name	Name
Address	Address
Phone Cell	Phone Cell
Office Fax	Office Fax
Email	Email

Name	Name
Address	Address
Phone Cell	Phone Cell
Office Fax	Office Fax
Email	Email

An unexamined life is not worth living. –Socrates

Name	*Name*
Address	*Address*
Phone *Cell*	*Phone* *Cell*
Office *Fax*	*Office* *Fax*
Email	*Email*
Name	*Name*
Address	*Address*
Phone *Cell*	*Phone* *Cell*
Office *Fax*	*Office* *Fax*
Email	*Email*
Name	*Name*
Address	*Address*
Phone *Cell*	*Phone* *Cell*
Office *Fax*	*Office* *Fax*
Email	*Email*
Name	*Name*
Address	*Address*
Phone *Cell*	*Phone* *Cell*
Office *Fax*	*Office* *Fax*
Email	*Email*
Name	*Name*
Address	*Address*
Phone *Cell*	*Phone* *Cell*
Office *Fax*	*Office* *Fax*
Email	*Email*

The person who says it cannot be done should not interrupt the person who is doing it. –Chinese Proverb

I

Name

Address

Phone — *Cell*

Office — *Fax*

Email

Name

Address

Phone — *Cell*

Office — *Fax*

Email

Name

Address

Phone — *Cell*

Office — *Fax*

Email

Name

Address

Phone — *Cell*

Office — *Fax*

Email

Name

Address

Phone — *Cell*

Office — *Fax*

Email

Name

Address

Phone — *Cell*

Office — *Fax*

Email

Name

Address

Phone — *Cell*

Office — *Fax*

Email

Name

Address

Phone — *Cell*

Office — *Fax*

Email

Name

Address

Phone — *Cell*

Office — *Fax*

Email

Name

Address

Phone — *Cell*

Office — *Fax*

Email

Boldness has genius, power and magic in it. –Johann Wolfgang von Goethe

Name	*Name*
Address	*Address*
Phone *Cell*	*Phone* *Cell*
Office *Fax*	*Office* *Fax*
Email	*Email*
Name	*Name*
Address	*Address*
Phone *Cell*	*Phone* *Cell*
Office *Fax*	*Office* *Fax*
Email	*Email*
Name	*Name*
Address	*Address*
Phone *Cell*	*Phone* *Cell*
Office *Fax*	*Office* *Fax*
Email	*Email*
Name	*Name*
Address	*Address*
Phone *Cell*	*Phone* *Cell*
Office *Fax*	*Office* *Fax*
Email	*Email*
Name	*Name*
Address	*Address*
Phone *Cell*	*Phone* *Cell*
Office *Fax*	*Office* *Fax*
Email	*Email*

Build your own dreams, or someone else will hire you to build theirs. –Farrah Gray

J

Name

Address

Phone   *Cell*

Office   *Fax*

Email

Name

Address

Phone   *Cell*

Office   *Fax*

Email

Name

Address

Phone   *Cell*

Office   *Fax*

Email

Name

Address

Phone   *Cell*

Office   *Fax*

Email

Name

Address

Phone   *Cell*

Office   *Fax*

Email

Name

Address

Phone   *Coll*

Office   *Fax*

Email

Name

Address

Phone   *Cell*

Office   *Fax*

Email

Name

Address

Phone   *Cell*

Office   *Fax*

Email

Name

Address

Phone   *Cell*

Office   *Fax*

Email

Name

Address

Phone   *Cell*

Office   *Fax*

Email

The best revenge is massive success. –Frank Sinatra

Name
Address

Phone   Cell
Office   Fax
Email

Name
Address

Phone   Cell
Office   Fax
Email

Name
Address

Phone   Cell
Office   Fax
Email

Name
Address

Phone   Cell
Office   Fax
Email

Name
Address

Phone   Cell
Office   Fax
Email

Name
Address

Phone   Cell
Office   Fax
Email

Name
Address

Phone   Cell
Office   Fax
Email

Name
Address

Phone   Cell
Office   Fax
Email

Name
Address

Phone   Cell
Office   Fax
Email

Name
Address

Phone   Cell
Office   Fax
Email

It does not matter how slowly you go as long as you do not stop. –Confucius

J

Name
Address

Phone   *Cell*
Office   *Fax*
Email

Name
Address

Phone   *Cell*
Office   *Fax*
Email

Name
Address

Phone   *Cell*
Office   *Fax*
Email

Name
Address

Phone   *Cell*
Office   *Fax*
Email

Name
Address

Phone   *Cell*
Office   *Fax*
Email

Name
Address

Phone   *Cell*
Office   *Fax*
Email

Name
Address

Phone   *Cell*
Office   *Fax*
Email

Name
Address

Phone   *Cell*
Office   *Fax*
Email

Name
Address

Phone   *Cell*
Office   *Fax*
Email

Name
Address

Phone   *Cell*
Office   *Fax*
Email

A friend is one who knows you and loves you just the same.
- Elbert Hubbard

Name	*Name*
Address	*Address*
Phone　　*Cell*	*Phone*　　*Cell*
Office　　*Fax*	*Office*　　*Fax*
Email	*Email*
Name	*Name*
Address	*Address*
Phone　　*Cell*	*Phone*　　*Cell*
Office　　*Fax*	*Office*　　*Fax*
Email	*Email*
Name	*Name*
Address	*Address*
Phone　　*Cell*	*Phone*　　*Cell*
Office　　*Fax*	*Office*　　*Fax*
Email	*Email*
Name	*Name*
Address	*Address*
Phone　　*Cell*	*Phone*　　*Cell*
Office　　*Fax*	*Office*　　*Fax*
Email	*Email*
Name	*Name*
Address	*Address*
Phone　　*Cell*	*Phone*　　*Cell*
Office　　*Fax*	*Office*　　*Fax*
Email	*Email*

Two persons cannot long be friends if they cannot forgive each other's little failings. - Jean de la Bruyere

K

Name	*Name*
Address	*Address*
Phone *Cell*	*Phone* *Cell*
Office *Fax*	*Office* *Fax*
Email	*Email*

Name	*Name*
Address	*Address*
Phone *Cell*	*Phone* *Cell*
Office *Fax*	*Office* *Fax*
Email	*Email*

Name	*Name*
Address	*Address*
Phone *Cell*	*Phone* *Cell*
Office *Fax*	*Office* *Fax*
Email	*Email*

Name	*Name*
Address	*Address*
Phone *Cell*	*Phone* *Cell*
Office *Fax*	*Office* *Fax*
Email	*Email*

Name	*Name*
Address	*Address*
Phone *Cell*	*Phone* *Cell*
Office *Fax*	*Office* *Fax*
Email	*Email*

Everything you've ever wanted is on the other side of fear. –George Addair

K

Name
Address

Phone   Cell
Office   Fax
Email

Name
Address

Phone   Cell
Office   Fax
Email

Name
Address

Phone   Cell
Office   Fax
Email

Name
Address

Phone   Cell
Office   Fax
Email

Name
Address

Phone   Cell
Office   Fax
Email

Name
Address

Phone   Cell
Office   Fax
Email

Name
Address

Phone   Cell
Office   Fax
Email

Name
Address

Phone   Cell
Office   Fax
Email

Name
Address

Phone   Cell
Office   Fax
Email

Name
Address

Phone   Cell
Office   Fax
Email

A real friend is one who walks in when the rest of the world walks out.
- Walter Winchell

Name

Address

Phone   Cell

Office   Fax

Email

Name

Address

Phone   Cell

Office   Fax

Email

Name

Address

Phone   Cell

Office   Fax

Email

Name

Address

Phone   Cell

Office   Fax

Email

Name

Address

Phone   Cell

Office   Fax

Email

Name

Address

Phone   Cell

Office   Fax

Email

Name

Address

Phone   Cell

Office   Fax

Email

Name

Address

Phone   Cell

Office   Fax

Email

Name

Address

Phone   Cell

Office   Fax

Email

Name

Address

Phone   Cell

Office   Fax

Email

Dream big and dare to fail. –Norman Vaughan

L

Name
Address

Phone   Cell
Office   Fax
Email

Name
Address

Phone   Cell
Office   Fax
Email

Name
Address

Phone   Cell
Office   Fax
Email

Name
Address

Phone   Cell
Office   Fax
Email

Name
Address

Phone   Cell
Office   Fax
Email

Name
Address

Phone   Cell
Office   Fax
Email

Name
Address

Phone   Cell
Office   Fax
Email

Name
Address

Phone   Cell
Office   Fax
Email

Name
Address

Phone   Cell
Office   Fax
Email

Name
Address

Phone   Cell
Office   Fax
Email

As iron sharpens iron, so a friend sharpens a friend. - King Solomon

L

Name	**Name**
Address	Address
Phone Cell	Phone Cell
Office Fax	Office Fax
Email	Email
Name	**Name**
Address	Address
Phone Cell	Phone Cell
Office Fax	Office Fax
Email	Email
Name	**Name**
Address	Address
Phone Cell	Phone Cell
Office Fax	Office Fax
Email	Email
Name	**Name**
Address	Address
Phone Cell	Phone Cell
Office Fax	Office Fax
Email	Email
Name	**Name**
Address	Address
Phone Cell	Phone Cell
Office Fax	Office Fax
Email	Email

Eros will have naked bodies; Friendship naked personalities. - C. S. Lewis

L

Name
Address

Phone   *Cell*
Office   *Fax*
Email

Name
Address

Phone   *Cell*
Office   *Fax*
Email

Name
Address

Phone   *Cell*
Office   *Fax*
Email

Name
Address

Phone   *Cell*
Office   *Fax*
Email

Name
Address

Phone   *Cell*
Office   *Fax*
Email

Name
Address

Phone   *Cell*
Office   *Fax*
Email

Name
Address

Phone   *Cell*
Office   *Fax*
Email

Name
Address

Phone   *Cell*
Office   *Fax*
Email

Name
Address

Phone   *Cell*
Office   *Fax*
Email

Name
Address

Phone   *Cell*
Office   *Fax*
Email

Eighty percent of success is showing up. –Woody Allen

L

Name

Address

Phone   *Cell*

Office   *Fax*

Email

Name

Address

Phone   *Cell*

Office   *Fax*

Email

Name

Address

Phone   *Cell*

Office   *Fax*

Email

Name

Address

Phone   *Cell*

Office   *Fax*

Email

Name

Address

Phone   *Cell*

Office   *Fax*

Email

Name

Address

Phone   *Cell*

Office   *Fax*

Email

Name

Address

Phone   *Cell*

Office   *Fax*

Email

Name

Address

Phone   *Cell*

Office   *Fax*

Email

Name

Address

Phone   *Cell*

Office   *Fax*

Email

Name

Address

Phone   *Cell*

Office   *Fax*

Email

Many a friendship, long, loyal, and self-sacrificing, rested at first on no thicker a foundation than a kind word.

Name

Address

Phone   Cell

Office   Fax

Email

Name

Address

Phone   Cell

Office   Fax

Email

Name

Address

Phone   Cell

Office   Fax

Email

Name

Address

Phone   Cell

Office   Fax

Email

Name

Address

Phone   Cell

Office   Fax

Email

Name

Address

Phone   Cell

Office   Fax

Email

Name

Address

Phone   Cell

Office   Fax

Email

Name

Address

Phone   Cell

Office   Fax

Email

Name

Address

Phone   Cell

Office   Fax

Email

Name

Address

Phone   Cell

Office   Fax

Email

There are no traffic jams along the extra mile. –Roger Staubach

Name	Name
Address	Address
Phone Cell	Phone Cell
Office Fax	Office Fax
Email	Email

Name	Name
Address	Address
Phone Cell	Phone Cell
Office Fax	Office Fax
Email	Email

Name	Name
Address	Address
Phone Cell	Phone Cell
Office Fax	Office Fax
Email	Email

Name	Name
Address	Address
Phone Cell	Phone Cell
Office Fax	Office Fax
Email	Email

Name	Name
Address	Address
Phone Cell	Phone Cell
Office Fax	Office Fax
Email	Email

It's not the years in your life that count. It's the life in your years. –Abraham Lincoln

Name
Address

Phone   Cell
Office   Fax
Email

Name
Address

Phone   Cell
Office   Fax
Email

Name
Address

Phone   Cell
Office   Fax
Email

Name
Address

Phone   Cell
Office   Fax
Email

Name
Address

Phone   Cell
Office   Fax
Email

Name
Address

Phone   Cell
Office   Fax
Email

Name
Address

Phone   Cell
Office   Fax
Email

Name
Address

Phone   Cell
Office   Fax
Email

Name
Address

Phone   Cell
Office   Fax
Email

Name
Address

Phone   Cell
Office   Fax
Email

Life is 10% what happens to me and 90% of how I react to it. –Charles Swindoll

Name

Address

Phone *Cell*
Office *Fax*
Email

Name

Address

Phone *Cell*
Office *Fax*
Email

Name

Address

Phone *Cell*
Office *Fax*
Email

Name

Address

Phone *Cell*
Office *Fax*
Email

Name

Address

Phone *Cell*
Office *Fax*
Email

Name

Address

Phone *Cell*
Office *Fax*
Email

Name

Address

Phone *Cell*
Office *Fax*
Email

Name

Address

Phone *Cell*
Office *Fax*
Email

Name

Address

Phone *Cell*
Office *Fax*
Email

Name

Address

Phone *Cell*
Office *Fax*
Email

I attribute my success to this: I never gave or took any excuse. –Florence Nightingale

M

Name
Address

Phone   Cell
Office   Fax
Email

Name
Address

Phone   Cell
Office   Fax
Email

Name
Address

Phone   Cell
Office   Fax
Email

Name
Address

Phone   Cell
Office   Fax
Email

Name
Address

Phone   Cell
Office   Fax
Email

Name
Address

Phone   Cell
Office   Fax
Email

Name
Address

Phone   Cell
Office   Fax
Email

Name
Address

Phone   Cell
Office   Fax
Email

Name
Address

Phone   Cell
Office   Fax
Email

Name
Address

Phone   Cell
Office   Fax
Email

If you want to lift yourself up, lift up someone else. –Booker T. Washington

N

Name

Address

Phone   Cell

Office   Fax

Email

Name

Address

Phone   Cell

Office   Fax

Email

Name

Address

Phone   Cell

Office   Fax

Email

Name

Address

Phone   Cell

Office   Fax

Email

Name

Address

Phone   Cell

Office   Fax

Email

Name

Address

Phone   Cell

Office   Fax

Email

Name

Address

Phone   Cell

Office   Fax

Email

Name

Address

Phone   Cell

Office   Fax

Email

Name

Address

Phone   Cell

Office   Fax

Email

Name

Address

Phone   Cell

Office   Fax

Email

Always keep your eyes open. Keep watching. Because whatever you see can inspire you. –Grace Coddington

Name	Name
Address	Address
Phone Cell	Phone Cell
Office Fax	Office Fax
Email	Email

Name	Name
Address	Address
Phone Cell	Phone Cell
Office Fax	Office Fax
Email	Email

Name	Name
Address	Address
Phone Cell	Phone Cell
Office Fax	Office Fax
Email	Email

Name	Name
Address	Address
Phone Cell	Phone Cell
Office Fax	Office Fax
Email	Email

Name	Name
Address	Address
Phone Cell	Phone Cell
Office Fax	Office Fax
Email	Email

Everything has beauty, but not everyone can see. –Confucius

N

Name

Address

Phone　　　　　*Cell*
Office　　　　　*Fax*
Email

Name

Address

Phone　　　　　*Cell*
Office　　　　　*Fax*
Email

Name

Address

Phone　　　　　*Cell*
Office　　　　　*Fax*
Email

Name

Address

Phone　　　　　*Cell*
Office　　　　　*Fax*
Email

Name

Address

Phone　　　　　*Cell*
Office　　　　　*Fax*
Email

Name

Address

Phone　　　　　*Cell*
Office　　　　　*Fax*
Email

Name

Address

Phone　　　　　*Cell*
Office　　　　　*Fax*
Email

Name

Address

Phone　　　　　*Cell*
Office　　　　　*Fax*
Email

Name

Address

Phone　　　　　*Cell*
Office　　　　　*Fax*
Email

Name

Address

Phone　　　　　*Cell*
Office　　　　　*Fax*
Email

A person who never made a mistake never tried anything new. – Albert Einstein

Name

Address

Phone   *Cell*

Office   *Fax*

Email

Name

Address

Phone   *Cell*

Office   *Fax*

Email

Name

Address

Phone   *Cell*

Office   *Fax*

Email

Name

Address

Phone   *Cell*

Office   *Fax*

Email

Name

Address

Phone   *Cell*

Office   *Fax*

Email

Name

Address

Phone   *Cell*

Office   *Fax*

Email

Name

Address

Phone   *Cell*

Office   *Fax*

Email

Name

Address

Phone   *Cell*

Office   *Fax*

Email

Name

Address

Phone   *Cell*

Office   *Fax*

Email

Name

Address

Phone   *Cell*

Office   *Fax*

Email

Believe you can and you're halfway there. –Theodore Roosevelt

O

Name
Address

Phone   *Cell*
Office   *Fax*
Email

Name
Address

Phone   *Cell*
Office   *Fax*
Email

Name
Address

Phone   *Cell*
Office   *Fax*
Email

Name
Address

Phone   *Cell*
Office   *Fax*
Email

Name
Address

Phone   *Cell*
Office   *Fax*
Email

Name
Address

Phone   *Cell*
Office   *Fax*
Email

Name
Address

Phone   *Cell*
Office   *Fax*
Email

Name
Address

Phone   *Cell*
Office   *Fax*
Email

Name
Address

Phone   *Cell*
Office   *Fax*
Email

Name
Address

Phone   *Cell*
Office   *Fax*
Email

Creativity is intelligence having fun. –Albert Einstein

O

Name

Address

Phone   *Cell*
Office   *Fax*
Email

Name

Address

Phone   *Cell*
Office   *Fax*
Email

Name

Address

Phone   *Cell*
Office   *Fax*
Email

Name

Address

Phone   *Cell*
Office   *Fax*
Email

Name

Address

Phone   *Cell*
Office   *Fax*
Email

Name

Address

Phone   *Cell*
Office   *Fax*
Email

Name

Address

Phone   *Cell*
Office   *Fax*
Email

Name

Address

Phone   *Cell*
Office   *Fax*
Email

Name

Address

Phone   *Cell*
Office   *Fax*
Email

Name

Address

Phone   *Cell*
Office   *Fax*
Email

Every strike brings me closer to the next home run. --Babe Ruth

O

Name

Address

Phone   *Cell*

Office   *Fax*

Email

Name

Address

Phone   *Cell*

Office   *Fax*

Email

Name

Address

Phone   *Cell*

Office   *Fax*

Email

Name

Address

Phone   *Cell*

Office   *Fax*

Email

Name

Address

Phone   *Cell*

Office   *Fax*

Email

Name

Address

Phone   *Cell*

Office   *Fax*

Email

Name

Address

Phone   *Cell*

Office   *Fax*

Email

Name

Address

Phone   *Cell*

Office   *Fax*

Email

Name

Address

Phone   *Cell*

Office   *Fax*

Email

Name

Address

Phone   *Cell*

Office   *Fax*

Email

Nothing is impossible, the word itself says, "I'm possible!" –Audrey Hepburn

Name		*Name*	
Address		*Address*	
Phone	*Cell*	*Phone*	*Cell*
Office	*Fax*	*Office*	*Fax*
Email		*Email*	

Name		*Name*	
Address		*Address*	
Phone	*Cell*	*Phone*	*Cell*
Office	*Fax*	*Office*	*Fax*
Email		*Email*	

Name		*Name*	
Address		*Address*	
Phone	*Cell*	*Phone*	*Cell*
Office	*Fax*	*Office*	*Fax*
Email		*Email*	

Name		*Name*	
Address		*Address*	
Phone	*Cell*	*Phone*	*Cell*
Office	*Fax*	*Office*	*Fax*
Email		*Email*	

Name		*Name*	
Address		*Address*	
Phone	*Cell*	*Phone*	*Cell*
Office	*Fax*	*Office*	*Fax*
Email		*Email*	

The language of friendship is not words but meanings. - Henry David Thoreau

Name

Address

Phone   *Cell*

Office   *Fax*

Email

Name

Address

Phone   *Cell*

Office   *Fax*

Email

Name

Address

Phone   *Cell*

Office   *Fax*

Email

Name

Address

Phone   *Cell*

Office   *Fax*

Email

Name

Address

Phone   *Cell*

Office   *Fax*

Email

Name

Address

Phone   *Cell*

Office   *Fax*

Email

Name

Address

Phone   *Cell*

Office   *Fax*

Email

Name

Address

Phone   *Cell*

Office   *Fax*

Email

Name

Address

Phone   *Cell*

Office   *Fax*

Email

Name

Address

Phone   *Cell*

Office   *Fax*

Email

Love is blind; friendship closes its eyes.
- Friedrich Nietzsche

P

Name

Address

Phone   *Cell*

Office   *Fax*

Email

Name

Address

Phone   *Cell*

Office   *Fax*

Email

Name

Address

Phone   *Cell*

Office   *Fax*

Email

Name

Address

Phone   *Cell*

Office   *Fax*

Email

Name

Address

Phone   *Cell*

Office   *Fax*

Email

Name

Address

Phone   *Cell*

Office   *Fax*

Email

Name

Address

Phone   *Cell*

Office   *Fax*

Email

Name

Address

Phone   *Cell*

Office   *Fax*

Email

Name

Address

Phone   *Cell*

Office   *Fax*

Email

Name

Address

Phone   *Cell*

Office   *Fax*

Email

Remember no one can make you feel inferior without your consent. –Eleanor Roosevelt

P

Name

Address

Phone   *Cell*

Office   *Fax*

Email

Name

Address

Phone   *Cell*

Office   *Fax*

Email

Name

Address

Phone   *Cell*

Office   *Fax*

Email

Name

Address

Phone   *Cell*

Office   *Fax*

Email

Name

Address

Phone   *Cell*

Office   *Fax*

Email

Name

Address

Phone   *Cell*

Office   *Fax*

Email

Name

Address

Phone   *Cell*

Office   *Fax*

Email

Name

Address

Phone   *Cell*

Office   *Fax*

Email

Name

Address

Phone   *Cell*

Office   *Fax*

Email

Name

Address

Phone   *Cell*

Office   *Fax*

Email

We become what we think about. –Earl Nightingale

P

Name

Address

Phone   Cell
Office   Fax
Email

Name

Address

Phone   Cell
Office   Fax
Email

Name

Address

Phone   Cell
Office   Fax
Email

Name

Address

Phone   Cell
Office   Fax
Email

Name

Address

Phone   Cell
Office   Fax
Email

Name

Address

Phone   Cell
Office   Fax
Email

Name

Address

Phone   Cell
Office   Fax
Email

Name

Address

Phone   Cell
Office   Fax
Email

Name

Address

Phone   Cell
Office   Fax
Email

Name

Address

Phone   Cell
Office   Fax
Email

It is never too late to be what you might have been. –George Eliot

P

Name

Address

Phone   Cell

Office   Fax

Email

Name

Address

Phone   Cell

Office   Fax

Email

Name

Address

Phone   Cell

Office   Fax

Email

Name

Address

Phone   Cell

Office   Fax

Email

Name

Address

Phone   Cell

Office   Fax

Email

Name

Address

Phone   Cell

Office   Fax

Email

Name

Address

Phone   Cell

Office   Fax

Email

Name

Address

Phone   Cell

Office   Fax

Email

Name

Address

Phone   Cell

Office   Fax

Email

Name

Address

Phone   Cell

Office   Fax

Email

Definiteness of purpose is the starting point of all achievement. –W. Clement Stone

Name	**Name**
Address	Address
Phone Cell	Phone Cell
Office Fax	Office Fax
Email	Email
Name	**Name**
Address	Address
Phone Cell	Phone Cell
Office Fax	Office Fax
Email	Email
Name	**Name**
Address	Address
Phone Cell	Phone Cell
Office Fax	Office Fax
Email	Email
Name	**Name**
Address	Address
Phone Cell	Phone Cell
Office Fax	Office Fax
Email	Email
Name	**Name**
Address	Address
Phone Cell	Phone Cell
Office Fax	Office Fax
Email	Email

The more you use, the more you have. –Maya Angelou

Q

Name

Address

Phone   Cell

Office   Fax

Email

Name

Address

Phone   Cell

Office   Fax

Email

Name

Address

Phone   Cell

Office   Fax

Email

Name

Address

Phone   Cell

Office   Fax

Email

Name

Address

Phone   Cell

Office   Fax

Email

Name

Address

Phone   Cell

Office   Fax

Email

Name

Address

Phone   Cell

Office   Fax

Email

Name

Address

Phone   Cell

Office   Fax

Email

Name

Address

Phone   Cell

Office   Fax

Email

Name

Address

Phone   Cell

Office   Fax

Email

The problem is how to remain an artist once he grows up. –Pablo Picasso

Name

Address

Phone   *Cell*

Office   *Fax*

Email

Name

Address

Phone   *Cell*

Office   *Fax*

Email

Name

Address

Phone   *Cell*

Office   *Fax*

Email

Name

Address

Phone   *Cell*

Office   *Fax*

Email

Name

Address

Phone   *Cell*

Office   *Fax*

Email

Name

Address

Phone   *Cell*

Office   *Fax*

Email

Name

Address

Phone   *Cell*

Office   *Fax*

Email

Name

Address

Phone   *Cell*

Office   *Fax*

Email

Name

Address

Phone   *Cell*

Office   *Fax*

Email

Name

Address

Phone   *Cell*

Office   *Fax*

Email

Life is what happens to you while you're busy making other plans. –John Lennon

R

Name
Address

Phone   Cell
Office   Fax
Email

Name
Address

Phone   Cell
Office   Fax
Email

Name
Address

Phone   Cell
Office   Fax
Email

Name
Address

Phone   Cell
Office   Fax
Email

Name
Address

Phone   Cell
Office   Fax
Email

Name
Address

Phone   Cell
Office   Fax
Email

Name
Address

Phone   Cell
Office   Fax
Email

Name
Address

Phone   Cell
Office   Fax
Email

Name
Address

Phone   Cell
Office   Fax
Email

Name
Address

Phone   Cell
Office   Fax
Email

Either write something worth reading or do something worth writing. –Benjamin Franklin

Name		*Name*	
Address		*Address*	
Phone	*Cell*	*Phone*	*Cell*
Office	*Fax*	*Office*	*Fax*
Email		*Email*	
Name		*Name*	
Address		*Address*	
Phone	*Cell*	*Phone*	*Cell*
Office	*Fax*	*Office*	*Fax*
Email		*Email*	
Name		*Name*	
Address		*Address*	
Phone	*Cell*	*Phone*	*Cell*
Office	*Fax*	*Office*	*Fax*
Email		*Email*	
Name		*Name*	
Address		*Address*	
Phone	*Cell*	*Phone*	*Cell*
Office	*Fax*	*Office*	*Fax*
Email		*Email*	
Name		*Name*	
Address		*Address*	
Phone	*Cell*	*Phone*	*Cell*
Office	*Fax*	*Office*	*Fax*
Email		*Email*	

You miss 100% of the shots you don't take. –Wayne Gretzky

Name

Address

Phone   *Cell*

Office   *Fax*

Email

Name

Address

Phone   *Cell*

Office   *Fax*

Email

Name

Address

Phone   *Cell*

Office   *Fax*

Email

Name

Address

Phone   *Cell*

Office   *Fax*

Email

Name

Address

Phone   *Cell*

Office   *Fax*

Email

Name

Address

Phone   *Cell*

Office   *Fax*

Email

Name

Address

Phone   *Cell*

Office   *Fax*

Email

Name

Address

Phone   *Cell*

Office   *Fax*

Email

Name

Address

Phone   *Cell*

Office   *Fax*

Email

Name

Address

Phone   *Cell*

Office   *Fax*

Email

A true friend is someone who is there for you when he'd rather be anywhere else. - Len Wein

R

Name

Address

Phone   *Cell*
Office   *Fax*
Email

Name

Address

Phone   *Cell*
Office   *Fax*
Email

Name

Address

Phone   *Cell*
Office   *Fax*
Email

Name

Address

Phone   *Cell*
Office   *Fax*
Email

Name

Address

Phone   *Cell*
Office   *Fax*
Email

Name

Address

Phone   *Cell*
Office   *Fax*
Email

Name

Address

Phone   *Cell*
Office   *Fax*
Email

Name

Address

Phone   *Cell*
Office   *Fax*
Email

Name

Address

Phone   *Cell*
Office   *Fax*
Email

Name

Address

Phone   *Cell*
Office   *Fax*
Email

Remember that not getting what you want is sometimes a wonderful stroke of luck. –Dalai Lama

Name

Address

Phone   Cell

Office   Fax

Email

Name

Address

Phone   Cell

Office   Fax

Email

Name

Address

Phone   Cell

Office   Fax

Email

Name

Address

Phone   Cell

Office   Fax

Email

Name

Address

Phone   Cell

Office   Fax

Email

Name

Address

Phone   Cell

Office   Fax

Email

Name

Address

Phone   Cell

Office   Fax

Email

Name

Address

Phone   Cell

Office   Fax

Email

Name

Address

Phone   Cell

Office   Fax

Email

Name

Address

Phone   Cell

Office   Fax

Email

Be slow in choosing a friend, slower in changing.
- Benjamin Franklin

Name

Address

Phone   *Cell*

Office   *Fax*

Email

Name

Address

Phone   *Cell*

Office   *Fax*

Email

Name

Address

Phone   *Cell*

Office   *Fax*

Email

Name

Address

Phone   *Cell*

Office   *Fax*

Email

Name

Address

Phone   *Cell*

Office   *Fax*

Email

Name

Address

Phone   *Cell*

Office   *Fax*

Email

Name

Address

Phone   *Cell*

Office   *Fax*

Email

Name

Address

Phone   *Cell*

Office   *Fax*

Email

Name

Address

Phone   *Cell*

Office   *Fax*

Email

Name

Address

Phone   *Cell*

Office   *Fax*

Email

Teach thy tongue to say, "I do not know," and thous shalt progress.
—Maimonides

S

Name

Address

Phone   *Cell*

Office   *Fax*

Email

Name

Address

Phone   *Cell*

Office   *Fax*

Email

Name

Address

Phone   *Cell*

Office   *Fax*

Email

Name

Address

Phone   *Cell*

Office   *Fax*

Email

Name

Address

Phone   *Cell*

Office   *Fax*

Email

Name

Address

Phone   *Cell*

Office   *Fax*

Email

Name

Address

Phone   *Cell*

Office   *Fax*

Email

Name

Address

Phone   *Cell*

Office   *Fax*

Email

Name

Address

Phone   *Cell*

Office   *Fax*

Email

Name

Address

Phone   *Cell*

Office   *Fax*

Email

When I let go of what I am, I become what I might be. –Lao Tzu

Name	*Name*
Address	*Address*
Phone　　　　　　*Cell*	*Phone*　　　　　　*Cell*
Office　　　　　　*Fax*	*Office*　　　　　　*Fax*
Email	*Email*
Name	*Name*
Address	*Address*
Phone　　　　　　*Cell*	*Phone*　　　　　　*Cell*
Office　　　　　　*Fax*	*Office*　　　　　　*Fax*
Email	*Email*
Name	*Name*
Address	*Address*
Phone　　　　　　*Cell*	*Phone*　　　　　　*Cell*
Office　　　　　　*Fax*	*Office*　　　　　　*Fax*
Email	*Email*
Name	*Name*
Address	*Address*
Phone　　　　　　*Cell*	*Phone*　　　　　　*Cell*
Office　　　　　　*Fax*	*Office*　　　　　　*Fax*
Email	*Email*
Name	*Name*
Address	*Address*
Phone　　　　　　*Cell*	*Phone*　　　　　　*Cell*
Office　　　　　　*Fax*	*Office*　　　　　　*Fax*
Email	*Email*

I didn't fail the test. I just found 100 ways to do it wrong. –Benjamin Franklin

S

Name

Address

Phone · Cell

Office · Fax

Email

Name

Address

Phone · Cell

Office · Fax

Email

Name

Address

Phone · Cell

Office · Fax

Email

Name

Address

Phone · Cell

Office · Fax

Email

Name

Address

Phone · Cell

Office · Fax

Email

Name

Address

Phone · Cell

Office · Fax

Email

Name

Address

Phone · Cell

Office · Fax

Email

Name

Address

Phone · Cell

Office · Fax

Email

Name

Address

Phone · Cell

Office · Fax

Email

Name

Address

Phone · Cell

Office · Fax

Email

Anyone who has ever made anything of importance was disciplined. –Andrew Hendrixson

Name

Address

Phone   Cell

Office   Fax

Email

Name

Address

Phone   Cell

Office   Fax

Email

Name

Address

Phone   Cell

Office   Fax

Email

Name

Address

Phone   Cell

Office   Fax

Email

Name

Address

Phone   Cell

Office   Fax

Email

Name

Address

Phone   Cell

Office   Fax

Email

Name

Address

Phone   Cell

Office   Fax

Email

Name

Address

Phone   Cell

Office   Fax

Email

Name

Address

Phone   Cell

Office   Fax

Email

Name

Address

Phone   Cell

Office   Fax

Email

It comes from your own actions. –Dalai Lama

S

Name

Address

Phone   *Cell*

Office   *Fax*

Email

Name

Address

Phone   *Cell*

Office   *Fax*

Email

Name

Address

Phone   *Cell*

Office   *Fax*

Email

Name

Address

Phone   *Cell*

Office   *Fax*

Email

Name

Address

Phone   *Cell*

Office   *Fax*

Email

Name

Address

Phone   *Cell*

Office   *Fax*

Email

Name

Address

Phone   *Cell*

Office   *Fax*

Email

Name

Address

Phone   *Cell*

Office   *Fax*

Email

Name

Address

Phone   *Cell*

Office   *Fax*

Email

Name

Address

Phone   *Cell*

Office   *Fax*

Email

No person is your friend who demands your silence, or denies your right to grow. - Alice Walker

Name		Name	
Address		Address	
Phone	Cell	Phone	Cell
Office	Fax	Office	Fax
Email		Email	

Name		Name	
Address		Address	
Phone	Cell	Phone	Cell
Office	Fax	Office	Fax
Email		Email	

Name		Name	
Address		Address	
Phone	Cell	Phone	Cell
Office	Fax	Office	Fax
Email		Email	

Name		Name	
Address		Address	
Phone	Cell	Phone	Cell
Office	Fax	Office	Fax
Email		Email	

Name		Name	
Address		Address	
Phone	Cell	Phone	Cell
Office	Fax	Office	Fax
Email		Email	

True friendship is like sound health; the value of it is seldom known until it is lost. - Charles Caleb Colton

T

Name

Address

Phone   Cell

Office   Fax

Email

Name

Address

Phone   Cell

Office   Fax

Email

Name

Address

Phone   Cell

Office   Fax

Email

Name

Address

Phone   Cell

Office   Fax

Email

Name

Address

Phone   Cell

Office   Fax

Email

Name

Address

Phone   Cell

Office   Fax

Email

Name

Address

Phone   Cell

Office   Fax

Email

Name

Address

Phone   Cell

Office   Fax

Email

Name

Address

Phone   Cell

Office   Fax

Email

Name

Address

Phone   Cell

Office   Fax

Email

A true friend is not the person who will kill for you, rather the one who will die for you.

Name	*Name*
Address	*Address*
Phone *Cell*	*Phone* *Cell*
Office *Fax*	*Office* *Fax*
Email	*Email*
Name	*Name*
Address	*Address*
Phone *Cell*	*Phone* *Cell*
Office *Fax*	*Office* *Fax*
Email	*Email*
Name	*Name*
Address	*Address*
Phone *Cell*	*Phone* *Cell*
Office *Fax*	*Office* *Fax*
Email	*Email*
Name	*Name*
Address	*Address*
Phone *Cell*	*Phone* *Cell*
Office *Fax*	*Office* *Fax*
Email	*Email*
Name	*Name*
Address	*Address*
Phone *Cell*	*Phone* *Cell*
Office *Fax*	*Office* *Fax*
Email	*Email*

But then so does ignorance. --Sir Claus Moser

T

Name

Address

Phone   Cell
Office   Fax
Email

Name

Address

Phone   Cell
Office   Fax
Email

Name

Address

Phone   Cell
Office   Fax
Email

Name

Address

Phone   Cell
Office   Fax
Email

Name

Address

Phone   Cell
Office   Fax
Email

Name

Address

Phone   Cell
Office   Fax
Email

Name

Address

Phone   Cell
Office   Fax
Email

Name

Address

Phone   Cell
Office   Fax
Email

Name

Address

Phone   Cell
Office   Fax
Email

Name

Address

Phone   Cell
Office   Fax
Email

Do what you can, where you are, with what you have. —Teddy Roosevelt

T

Name		Name	
Address		Address	
Phone	Cell	Phone	Cell
Office	Fax	Office	Fax
Email		Email	

Name		Name	
Address		Address	
Phone	Cell	Phone	Cell
Office	Fax	Office	Fax
Email		Email	

Name		Name	
Address		Address	
Phone	Cell	Phone	Cell
Office	Fax	Office	Fax
Email		Email	

Name		Name	
Address		Address	
Phone	Cell	Phone	Cell
Office	Fax	Office	Fax
Email		Email	

Name		Name	
Address		Address	
Phone	Cell	Phone	Cell
Office	Fax	Office	Fax
Email		Email	

15.Life is 10% what happens to me and 90% of how I react to it. —Charles Swindoll

T

Name

Address

Phone   *Cell*

Office   *Fax*

Email

Name

Address

Phone   *Cell*

Office   *Fax*

Email

Name

Address

Phone   *Cell*

Office   *Fax*

Email

Name

Address

Phone   *Cell*

Office   *Fax*

Email

Name

Address

Phone   *Cell*

Office   *Fax*

Email

Name

Address

Phone   *Cell*

Office   *Fax*

Email

Name

Address

Phone   *Cell*

Office   *Fax*

Email

Name

Address

Phone   *Cell*

Office   *Fax*

Email

Name

Address

Phone   *Cell*

Office   *Fax*

Email

Name

Address

Phone   *Cell*

Office   *Fax*

Email

Friendship often ends in love; but love in friendship - never.

Name		Name	
Address		Address	
Phone	Cell	Phone	Cell
Office	Fax	Office	Fax
Email		Email	

Name		Name	
Address		Address	
Phone	Cell	Phone	Cell
Office	Fax	Office	Fax
Email		Email	

Name		Name	
Address		Address	
Phone	Cell	Phone	Cell
Office	Fax	Office	Fax
Email		Email	

Name		Name	
Address		Address	
Phone	Cell	Phone	Cell
Office	Fax	Office	Fax
Email		Email	

Name		Name	
Address		Address	
Phone	Cell	Phone	Cell
Office	Fax	Office	Fax
Email		Email	

There is only one way to avoid criticism: do nothing, say nothing, and be nothing. –Aristotle

Name	Name
Address	Address
Phone Cell	Phone Cell
Office Fax	Office Fax
Email	Email

Name	Name
Address	Address
Phone Cell	Phone Cell
Office Fax	Office Fax
Email	Email

Name	Name
Address	Address
Phone Cell	Phone Cell
Office Fax	Office Fax
Email	Email

Name	Name
Address	Address
Phone Cell	Phone Cell
Office Fax	Office Fax
Email	Email

Name	Name
Address	Address
Phone Cell	Phone Cell
Office Fax	Office Fax
Email	Email

Change your thoughts and you change your world. –Norman Vincent Peale

U

Name		*Name*	
Address		*Address*	
Phone	*Cell*	*Phone*	*Cell*
Office	*Fax*	*Office*	*Fax*
Email		*Email*	

Name		*Name*	
Address		*Address*	
Phone	*Cell*	*Phone*	*Cell*
Office	*Fax*	*Office*	*Fax*
Email		*Email*	

Name		*Name*	
Address		*Address*	
Phone	*Cell*	*Phone*	*Cell*
Office	*Fax*	*Office*	*Fax*
Email		*Email*	

Name		*Name*	
Address		*Address*	
Phone	*Cell*	*Phone*	*Cell*
Office	*Fax*	*Office*	*Fax*
Email		*Email*	

Name		*Name*	
Address		*Address*	
Phone	*Cell*	*Phone*	*Cell*
Office	*Fax*	*Office*	*Fax*
Email		*Email*	

You become what you believe. –Oprah Winfrey

V

Name

Address

Phone   *Cell*

Office   *Fax*

Email

Name

Address

Phone   *Cell*

Office   *Fax*

Email

Name

Address

Phone   *Cell*

Office   *Fax*

Email

Name

Address

Phone   *Cell*

Office   *Fax*

Email

Name

Address

Phone   *Cell*

Office   *Fax*

Email

Name

Address

Phone   *Cell*

Office   *Fax*

Email

Name

Address

Phone   *Cell*

Office   *Fax*

Email

Name

Address

Phone   *Cell*

Office   *Fax*

Email

Name

Address

Phone   *Cell*

Office   *Fax*

Email

Name

Address

Phone   *Cell*

Office   *Fax*

Email

Life is what we make it, always has been, always will be. --Grandma Moses

V

Name	*Name*
Address	*Address*
Phone *Cell*	*Phone* *Cell*
Office *Fax*	*Office* *Fax*
Email	*Email*
Name	*Name*
Address	*Address*
Phone *Cell*	*Phone* *Cell*
Office *Fax*	*Office* *Fax*
Email	*Email*
Name	*Name*
Address	*Address*
Phone *Cell*	*Phone* *Cell*
Office *Fax*	*Office* *Fax*
Email	*Email*
Name	*Name*
Address	*Address*
Phone *Cell*	*Phone* *Cell*
Office *Fax*	*Office* *Fax*
Email	*Email*
Name	*Name*
Address	*Address*
Phone *Cell*	*Phone* *Cell*
Office *Fax*	*Office* *Fax*
Email	*Email*

Your time is limited, so don't waste it living someone else's life. –Steve Jobs

W

Name

Address

Phone　　　　　*Cell*

Office　　　　　*Fax*

Email

Name

Address

Phone　　　　　*Cell*

Office　　　　　*Fax*

Email

Name

Address

Phone　　　　　*Cell*

Office　　　　　*Fax*

Email

Name

Address

Phone　　　　　*Cell*

Office　　　　　*Fax*

Email

Name

Address

Phone　　　　　*Cell*

Office　　　　　*Fax*

Email

Name

Address

Phone　　　　　*Cell*

Office　　　　　*Fax*

Email

Name

Address

Phone　　　　　*Cell*

Office　　　　　*Fax*

Email

Name

Address

Phone　　　　　*Cell*

Office　　　　　*Fax*

Email

Name

Address

Phone　　　　　*Cell*

Office　　　　　*Fax*

Email

Name

Address

Phone　　　　　*Cell*

Office　　　　　*Fax*

Email

A friend is someone who knows the song in your heart and can sing it back to you when you have forgotten the words.

Name	
Address	

Phone	Cell
Office	Fax
Email	

Name	
Address	

Phone	Cell
Office	Fax
Email	

Name	
Address	

Phone	Cell
Office	Fax
Email	

Name	
Address	

Phone	Cell
Office	Fax
Email	

Name	
Address	

Phone	Cell
Office	Fax
Email	

Name	
Address	

Phone	Cell
Office	Fax
Email	

Name	
Address	

Phone	Cell
Office	Fax
Email	

Name	
Address	

Phone	Cell
Office	Fax
Email	

Name	
Address	

Phone	Cell
Office	Fax
Email	

Name	
Address	

Phone	Cell
Office	Fax
Email	

Too many of us are not living our dreams because we are living our fears. –Les Brown

Name

Address

Phone   *Cell*

Office   *Fax*

Email

Name

Address

Phone   *Cell*

Office   *Fax*

Email

Name

Address

Phone   *Cell*

Office   *Fax*

Email

Name

Address

Phone   *Cell*

Office   *Fax*

Email

Name

Address

Phone   *Cell*

Office   *Fax*

Email

Name

Address

Phone   *Cell*

Office   *Fax*

Email

Name

Address

Phone   *Cell*

Office   *Fax*

Email

Name

Address

Phone   *Cell*

Office   *Fax*

Email

Name

Address

Phone   *Cell*

Office   *Fax*

Email

Name

Address

Phone   *Cell*

Office   *Fax*

Email

Anyone can make you smile or cry but it takes someone special to make you smile when you already have tears in your eyes.

W

Name	Name
Address	Address
Phone Cell	Phone Cell
Office Fax	Office Fax
Email	Email

Name	Name
Address	Address
Phone Cell	Phone Cell
Office Fax	Office Fax
Email	Email

Name	Name
Address	Address
Phone Cell	Phone Cell
Office Fax	Office Fax
Email	Email

Name	Name
Address	Address
Phone Cell	Phone Cell
Office Fax	Office Fax
Email	Email

Name	Name
Address	Address
Phone Cell	Phone Cell
Office Fax	Office Fax
Email	Email

A good friend is like a four-leaf clover; hard to find and lucky to have.

X

Name

Address

Phone   *Cell*
Office   *Fax*
Email

Name

Address

Phone   *Cell*
Office   *Fax*
Email

Name

Address

Phone   *Cell*
Office   *Fax*
Email

Name

Address

Phone   *Cell*
Office   *Fax*
Email

Name

Address

Phone   *Cell*
Office   *Fax*
Email

Name

Address

Phone   *Cell*
Office   *Fax*
Email

Name

Address

Phone   *Cell*
Office   *Fax*
Email

Name

Address

Phone   *Cell*
Office   *Fax*
Email

Name

Address

Phone   *Cell*
Office   *Fax*
Email

Name

Address

Phone   *Cell*
Office   *Fax*
Email

The greatest gift of life is friendship, and I have received it.
- Hubert H. Humphrey

X

Name		Name	
Address		Address	
Phone	Cell	Phone	Cell
Office	Fax	Office	Fax
Email		Email	

Name		Name	
Address		Address	
Phone	Cell	Phone	Cell
Office	Fax	Office	Fax
Email		Email	

Name		Name	
Address		Address	
Phone	Cell	Phone	Cell
Office	Fax	Office	Fax
Email		Email	

Name		Name	
Address		Address	
Phone	Cell	Phone	Cell
Office	Fax	Office	Fax
Email		Email	

Name		Name	
Address		Address	
Phone	Cell	Phone	Cell
Office	Fax	Office	Fax
Email		Email	

The most difficult thing is the decision to act, the rest is merely tenacity.
–Amelia Earhart

Y

Name

Address

Phone *Cell*

Office *Fax*

Email

Name

Address

Phone *Cell*

Office *Fax*

Email

Name

Address

Phone *Cell*

Office *Fax*

Email

Name

Address

Phone *Cell*

Office *Fax*

Email

Name

Address

Phone *Cell*

Office *Fax*

Email

Name

Address

Phone *Cell*

Office *Fax*

Email

Name

Address

Phone *Cell*

Office *Fax*

Email

Name

Address

Phone *Cell*

Office *Fax*

Email

Name

Address

Phone *Cell*

Office *Fax*

Email

Name

Address

Phone *Cell*

Office *Fax*

Email

Life isn't about getting and having, it's about giving and being. –Kevin Kruse

Y

Name		Name	
Address		Address	
Phone	Cell	Phone	Cell
Office	Fax	Office	Fax
Email		Email	

Name		Name	
Address		Address	
Phone	Cell	Phone	Cell
Office	Fax	Office	Fax
Email		Email	

Name		Name	
Address		Address	
Phone	Cell	Phone	Cell
Office	Fax	Office	Fax
Email		Email	

Name		Name	
Address		Address	
Phone	Cell	Phone	Cell
Office	Fax	Office	Fax
Email		Email	

Name		Name	
Address		Address	
Phone	Cell	Phone	Cell
Office	Fax	Office	Fax
Email		Email	

Our lives begin to end the day we become silent about things that matter.
—Martin Luther King Jr.

Z

Name	*Name*
Address	*Address*
Phone *Cell*	*Phone* *Cell*
Office *Fax*	*Office* *Fax*
Email	*Email*
Name	*Name*
Address	*Address*
Phone *Cell*	*Phone* *Cell*
Office *Fax*	*Office* *Fax*
Email	*Email*
Name	*Name*
Address	*Address*
Phone *Cell*	*Phone* *Cell*
Office *Fax*	*Office* *Fax*
Email	*Email*
Name	*Name*
Address	*Address*
Phone *Cell*	*Phone* *Cell*
Office *Fax*	*Office* *Fax*
Email	*Email*
Name	*Name*
Address	*Address*
Phone *Cell*	*Phone* *Cell*
Office *Fax*	*Office* *Fax*
Email	*Email*

You take your life in your own hands, and what happens? A terrible thing, no one to blame. –Erica Jong

Z

Name

Address

Phone   Cell
Office   Fax
Email

Name

Address

Phone   Cell
Office   Fax
Email

Name

Address

Phone   Cell
Office   Fax
Email

Name

Address

Phone   Cell
Office   Fax
Email

Name

Address

Phone   Cell
Office   Fax
Email

Name

Address

Phone   Cell
Office   Fax
Email

Name

Address

Phone   Cell
Office   Fax
Email

Name

Address

Phone   Cell
Office   Fax
Email

Name

Address

Phone   Cell
Office   Fax
Email

Name

Address

Phone   Cell
Office   Fax
Email

The best time to plant a tree was 20 years ago. The second best time is now.
—Chinese Proverb

For amazing journals and adult coloring books
from RW Squared Media, visit:

Amazon.com

CreateSpace.com

RWSquaredMedia.WordPress.com

She Believed She Could
So She Did
Adult Coloring Book

The Matryoshka Nesting Doll
Coloring Book for Adults

BONUS!!!

Link to download free PDF version of
"Color Your Butterflies Away"

RWSquaredmedia.wordpress.com/free-coloring-book/

Made in the USA
Columbia, SC
06 February 2022

55556601R00063